Here's How to Make Money Online

Money Online

By Paul Dot Net

About the Author

My name is Paul Dot Net. I am a full-time successful Internet Entrepreneur who makes a living on the Internet. I was born in Manchester, England where I spent most of my life before recently deciding to relocate to the Cote d'Azur.

My experiences as an Internet entrepreneur are what drove me to start writing books, so that I could give a little something back to society and also help others to achieve success.

I have always had a passion for reading books and firmly believe in the notion of gaining knowledge by reading. My passion for reading and always wanting to know more have driven me to online success, so I always recommend that people read more.

I came from a large family with four brothers and sisters. I was raised by my mother. Money was not readily available, and I believe this also contributed to my desire to succeed in life.

I left school with no qualifications, despite ranking at the top of my class with many subjects. I had an attitude problem and didn't realize how smart I actually was.

I went to college to study "just to prove to myself that I could have easily passed in school," then went on to a University, where I enrolled in a business studies degree course.

I dropped out to start my own car valeting business in Lancashire, England, and ran it successfully before embarking on my Internet career.

I was introduced to Internet Marketing by two friends who were very successful at what they did. I owe all of my success to their willingness to help me out. They gave me the necessary information I needed.

Now I want to help you out. I am living proof that you can succeed in making money online, despite my background, experience, or qualifications. You do not need to be a genius to succeed online. You just need belief in yourself.

Trust me. What you read in this book will change your life the way it changed mine.

Remember this as you read: "The best things do not come to those who wait; they come to those who go and take them."

Enjoy.

Table of Contents

Introduction

If you're reading this book, I assume you are looking for a way to make money online. You may be unemployed, underemployed, or employed full time. No matter what your employment status is, you know that the Internet is where the money is. You probably base this on the fact that so many people have gotten online and are making a fortune. You want to have a piece of that fortune as well. The problem is deciding what type of business to get into. That is where this book comes in.

Before the Internet, if you wanted to start a business, you would get a license from the county or city and then advertise in the local paper. You might even spread flyers around to let people know where your business is located. Once you put up your sign, people would come and check your

1

shop out to see what you have to offer. If you ran a service-related business, you could put a sign up, letting people know the service or services you provided.

You can make good money with a conventional business, especially if you live in a good area. However, with the recession and the economic troubles today, many such businesses are not doing as well as they want to/used to. This is particularly true for local businesses. However, the Internet has changed the way we can make money. You no longer have to focus on just your local community. You can actually spread out your business globally. It just takes the right idea and promoting yourself at the right places, and you can make a good living online.

With the use of the Internet, you are not confined to selling local. You can establish your online presence and sell around the world. If you do have a business and wish to take it online, you just need to create a website that features the products you sell or the services you provide. Once you have done that, the next step is to let people know about your website, getting your website in the front of people. You do this by way of Internet marketing.

In case you are not familiar with it, Internet marketing is a process where you spread your name, business, website, or whatever you are promoting online, connecting with your customers. The idea behind Internet marketing is to create a message about your business or website and get it to places where your future customers can read it.

Internet marketing is like conventional marketing, except you don't have the same channels to work with. Instead, you can create banners or small ads and ask certain websites to show those ads. Most business people hire Double-Click or another ad-serving company to place ads on certain high-traffic websites.

Other ways to get the message to people include using AdWords or other Pay-Per-Click systems. If you are not familiar with PPC, this is where you pay a certain price for certain keywords. When someone types in that keyword in the search results field, your ad will show up at the top or on the right-hand side. When people see the ad and click on it, it will take them to your website.

There are other ways to market your products and services online. You can place ads in Craigslist. You can join groups that talk about your industry. Once you have lurked for a while, you can read comments and answer them.

Be sure you include a link in your signature file, so when people see it, they will be enticed to click the link and land on your website. You can also sign up with many social media sites. By joining social sites, you'll have the opportunity to talk about your business and your site. If you make your post and comments interesting enough, you'll start seeing traffic that way as well.

There are many ways to promote your business or website. It is always good to know how to market your business, but for this book, the focus will be on the type of businesses you can start or find that will make you money. You can always look up Internet marketing on Google and find plenty of resources out there to help you find the information you needed.

However, what if you don't have a business to bring to the Internet. That shouldn't stop you from making money. There are several other ways you can make money online. Much of the material that is out there provides some ways to make money, but doesn't go into how to do it. I also have many years of experience in Internet marketing and running my own businesses. As such, I want to make sure you understand the various ways to make money online. I will explain what these methods are. I will also include an action plan so that you can take what I teach you and use it quickly. This is really the best way to get you started in making money online.

Keep this thought in mind. As you work each method, you may hear of people doing the same thing but getting better results. This doesn't mean you are doing anything wrong. It is just that your results may be different. That person may have heard about the methods and started on them a lot earlier than you started. Don't worry about what others are doing. Instead, focus on what you can do. There is plenty of money to go around; why not get your share?

As you learn each method, try one or many on a regular basis. The best way to succeed online is to start one effort and get that going and established before going on to the next one. Keep doing this with each one. Before you know it, you will have multiple income streams.

The only way for you to find which approaches work for you is to try each one. If you pick one that works, go for another one. There is nothing wrong with having multiple streams of passive income if you can get it. The goal is to make money online.

By the way, as you work each method, you may find one or more that you become more passionate about. If this happens, use it to your advantage and work those businesses fully. Once they are up and running 100%, you can go on and work other businesses. Any time a person goes after a passion, that person usually not only enjoys the process, but also is willing to work harder to succeed.

Identifying Your Niche

Before you decide which Internet business to get into, decide which niche or niches you want to focus on. The best Internet marketers usually focus on one or more niches. They focus on one niche first, work that, and then choose another one after. These niches should be those with little competition. If you go after low competition niches, you may find they will be great money makers.

There are many great niches mentioned in this book. However, if after you have gone through them, you don't find any that you like to work with, you'll need to understand niche marketing so that you can find your own niche to work with. You may even choose to work all the niches I have provided for you in this book and still want to find your own niche. For these reasons, it would be an excellent idea to learn about niche marketing.

How do you recognize a good niche? One great way is to examine your hobbies and interests as business opportunities. You don't have to know too much about the hobby or interest at first. You can do research. The best research is to type in the name of the hobby or interest in Google and see how many sites come up that feature that keyword on their pages.

For example, let's say your hobby is coin collecting. This is to general a niche. If you type in "coin collector" into Google, you will get over thirteen million results. Thus, this is not a good niche in which to belong. However, what if you narrowed it down to rare coin collector. I typed this phrase in and received 636,000 websites. This is a tighter niche, but one that is workable.

Do you see how this works? To find your niche, ask yourself these questions:

- What are your interests?

- What are you good at?

- Where is the demand?

- What can you contribute that people will find worth buying from you?

Remember that you have to identify something where there isn't a lot of competition. This is a niche where you can make a lot of money. Once you identify your niche, you have to find out what the major need is. You can do this by going to groups that are in that niche, and learn from others what product or service they need the most. Once you have identified the need, it is time to create the product or service to meet that need.

The secret to making good money from a niche is by selecting the right niche and beating your competition. In fact, like a spy, you should seek out what your competition is doing. Once you've identified your competition, learn about his/her product. It is important to learn the good and bad about it so that you can create a product that provides better results. It is when you provide a product that overcomes the weakness of your competition's product, that you'll be successful in selling it.

As an Internet marketer and businessman, your main goal in developing your product is to create a USP (unique selling proposition). When you have accomplished this, you will have created a product, with a marketing message that stands out from the crowd.

Making money online is not just about your passion and interest. It is also about doing something you love, and something that you can enjoy doing.

Tools You Can Use

If you are interested in finding a niche beyond what I provide for you in this book, you will need help in looking for one. There are tools you can use to assist you in your efforts. The best tool may be the keyword research tool. There are several that are available:

1. Wordtracker: With Wordtracker, there is a seven day trial version, and then you have to pay $59 a month. Wordtracker also provides a free tool to try out first, which can be accessed at https://freekeywords.wordtracker.com/.

2. Keyword Discovery: If you want a more comprehensive and analysis of keywords, consider Keyword Discovery. Get to them by going to http://www.keyworddiscovery.com/. This discovery tool pulls information from 200 search engines. The site also includes a great keyword research tool.

3. Google's AdWords Free Keyword Tool: You can use it whether or not you're logged into AdWords. If you do have an account with AdWords, you can log in and avoid the Captcha. The URL to access the tool is: https://adwords.google.com/o/Targeting/Explorer?_c=3476429307&_u=14383265078&_o=cues&ideaRequestType=KEYWORD_IDEAS.

Most Internet marketers use Wordtracker and Google's Free Keyword Tool, as these are the best around. They are quite thorough. Those who pay to use Wordtracker, however, know that the results they'll receive after creating their website pay for the monthly fee.

To use any of these keyword tools, you must enter a keyword based on your passion or interest. From that, the program will provide a list of keywords. Look through these keywords and find those of interest that have high hit rates.

For example, if you have a passion for skiing, type this word into the keyword tool. The next step is to combine your passion or interest word with words that will generate what is referred to as the problem statement, like "how to ski." Write down several of these words. These words are known by Internet marketers as "action words."

15

After you have written down a number of action words, decide the ones you like the most. Take that list and put them back into the keyword search tool. You'll get another list of results to look at.

Each time you enter a keyword phrase, you are creating a level of results. When you first began by typing in the action word along with the interest word, you reached the first level. When you typed in a combination action and interest word into the keyword tool, you reached level two. Each time you do a search using a keyword phrase from the previous level, you go deeper to another level.

Some Internet marketers go as many as seven levels and stop. They look at the list of keyword phrases they collected and set aside the top 25. Once they have the 25 top keyword phrases, they look at the list to determine which phrases they like the most and use them.

After you've done the research to find your niche, you can set up a business using the keyword phrases you found.

Top Niches That Are Proven Money Makers

Are you ready to find your niche within the pages of this book? So far, I've shown you how to find a niche market on your own. In the upcoming pages, I will provide you information on various niches that have been known to bring in a lot of money for those who've tried them.

With each niche, I will introduce an action plan you can use to set up your niche quickly. You won't have to wait until you read this book to get started. The action plan will guide you to the steps you have to take to implement that particular niche.

If you are ready, let's go...

1.0. Sell Affiliate Products

If you don't have your own product, you can still make money online by being an affiliate. This is someone who sells a product created by someone else. For instance, if you see Tom selling a book about rare coins, and he is doing exceptionally well with the book, you may offer to help sell the book for him with a guaranteed commission price for each sale. You are acting as the affiliate for Tom. When you sell Tom's book, Tom will pay you a small percentage or commission, for selling the book for him.

There are three types of affiliate programs available: pay-per-sale, pay-per-click, and pay-per-lead. Each one pays according to how the owner sets it up.

If you do not know any business person who is offering such a program, you can always get involved in affiliate sales by going to Commission Junction or Linkshare and find products that interest you. These sites offer many more merchants than you may find on your own.

Once you have decided on the product or products to sell, you have to let people know you are selling them. There are several ways you can do this:

1. Banner ads: A banner ad is a rectangular shaped box filled with information about a product, along with an image and a link. Banner ads are most commonly placed at the top of websites, but it is not uncommon to see them elsewhere on a site as well.

2. Product images: Some product owners will supply their own images

for you to use on your site. This is most practical, as they know how they want to convey the image of their products.

3. Text links: A text link is probably set up as an anchor text. For example, www.domainname.com is the actual website name. When you click the link, you will go to that site. This is known as an absolute link or URL. An anchor text link goes something like this: Domain Names. Do you notice the word "Domain Names" is in blue and underlined? This is referred to as an anchor text.

4. E-zine ads: E-zine ads are classified ads that are found in e-zines. These are electronic magazines. If the ad is well written where it forces the reader to take action, the reader will click the link in the ad.

5. E-mail promotions: E-mail promotions are campaigns set up to be delivered to certain people at a given time. The only ones to get such e-mail message are those who have asked to receive the e-mail.

6. Pop-ups: A pop-up is a small window that comes up on a computer screen. You can use it to advertise your affiliate product.

7. Product reviews: Product reviews are opinion pieces that describe or rate a certain product. Many people review products and provide a written summary of what they thought of the product, how it works for them, etc.

8. Articles: Articles are the best way to get traffic to your site. You can write about the product you are selling or about the industry for the product. Then you can submit the article or

articles to an article database. When people see the article, and they read it, they will click the link in the article and end up on your product site.

9. Interviews: You can even provide interviews on your site. Your seller can give you a link or a transcript that your visitors can read to provide proof that the product is well known.

10. Newsgroup posts: Another method of advertising your seller's product is by going to advertising newsgroups. You don't want to just go to any newsgroup and do this or you will be kicked out. You want to pick a newsgroup that allows advertising.

When you are setting up your site as an affiliate, don't skip on the design. Create a nice looking website that will attract and keep people interested in your site. The site you create should have value and be designed to highlight the program you are selling in its best light.

If you are looking to get involved in affiliate programs, make sure the product you want to help promote has been a proven moneymaker. If it isn't, you could be wasting your time promoting it, as you won't make any money from it.

If you can't find any programs to join at Commission Junction or at Linkshare.com, there are many other programs you might want to look into. These programs include:

- **Admob.com (http://www.google.com/ads/admob/)** - Admob is a company that specializes in providing ads for mobile tools. If you have a mobile web site, you can use this program to advertise on your site. This site is owned by Google. When ads show up in your

24

tool, and someone clicks the ad, you make money.

- **Clickbank.com**
  (http://www.clickbank.com) – Most every Internet marketer knows Clickbank, known as an affiliate website. Most marketers provide their products on Clickbank, as they know it is a place where others can help sell their products. Clickbank.com is the biggest affiliate website online today.

- **Gamestop.com**
  (http://www.gamestop.com/) – This website sells x-box and other video games. They also have an affiliate program. You may not make as much money as you would with other affiliate programs, but you still get your good amount.

- **Maxbounty.com**
  (http://www.maxbounty.com) -

Affiliates with Maxbounty earn money from advertising sponsors on a pay for performance basis. Maxbounty represents hundreds of advertisers and thousands of affiliate publishers as one of the largest and most experienced lead generation networks in the marketplace today.

- **Friendfinder.com (http://www.friendfinder.com)** – Friendfinder.com has one of the best affiliate programs online. You are paid for referring people to the owner's site, and for when the people sign up.

- **Liquidweb.com (http://www.liquidweb.com/)** - Liquid web has an awesome affiliate program. Their affiliate program is very straight forward. They pay the affiliate based on the type of account the referral picks.

- **Amazon.com
  (http://www.amazon.com)** – Most
  everyone knows about Amazon.
  However, not many know Amazon has
  a great affiliate program where you
  can sell items from others on their
  site.

1.1. Start Your Own Affiliate Program

So far, I spoke about how to sell products
created by other people. Now I'm going to
describe how you can make money getting
people to help sell your products. Why
should you focus strictly on selling a product
by someone else, when you can control the
amount of money you make by creating
your own product and hiring others to sell it
for you?

When you are setting up your first affiliate
product, there is something you will have

two choices. You can offer a one-tier or two-tier affiliate program.

In a one-tier affiliate program, you pay a commission to those who sell for you. These will be your affiliates. With a two-tier program, you have a bunch of regular affiliates selling for you, but those affiliates can hire their own affiliates to sell for them. These are known as sub-affiliates. Under the two-tier program, you will pay a commission to both the affiliates and sub-affiliates.

From a financial standpoint, you may want to think about which tier is better. Below are samples of what you can make when working with a tier one program as opposed to a tier two program.

Example #1: One-tier affiliates

You have June selling for you. You are paying her a commission of $10 for every $79 sale she sends your way.

For the first month, June was able to refer to you 16 customers. Here's how it looks broken down:

June's sales	**16 x $79 = $1264**
June's commission	**16 x $10 = $160**
This goes in your pocket!	**$1264 - $160 = $1104**

Example #2: Two-tier affiliates

In this example, you have June making $10 commission. However, June managed to

29

hire three affiliates to sell under her, so you have June as your affiliate and her three affiliates as your sub-affiliates. For every sale made by June's sub-affiliates, you'll pay June $3 as well as the standard $10 commission to the sub-affiliate who made the sale.

In the first month, June successfully recruits three new sub-affiliates. June is able to refer 16 people who made a purchase. Her sub-affiliates were able to produce 3, 5, and 6 sales each.

Take a look on the next page how this is all broken down.

	Sales ($79	Commissions ($10 per sale)
June	**16**	**$160**
Sub-Affiliate 1	**3**	**$30**
Sub-Affiliate 2	**5**	**$50**
Sub-Affiliate 3	**6**	**$60**
June's Sub-Affiliate referral fee ($3 per Sub-Affiliate sale, 14		**$42**
TOTAL AFFILIATE FEES PAYABLE		**$342**
YOUR TOTAL REVENUE	**30 x $79**	**$2,370**
THIS GOES IN YOUR POCKET	**$2,370 - $342**	**$2,028**

If you look carefully at the results, you may have noticed you made more money with your two-tier program, because even though you paid out more in commissions, you were able to make more as well. You didn't do any extra work but still made more money.

If you were to get into a three-tier program, June's sub-affiliates could sign up affiliates of their own. This may mean more commissions for you, but you also make a ton more in sales.

1.2. Using the Right Pay Model

Once you have decided on the tier program you want to go with, it is time to decide how you will pay your affiliates. There are three ways you can pay: sales, clicks, or leads.

If you decide to go with pay-per-sale, you will only pay your affiliates when a sale is made. If you went with pay-per-click, you would have to pay your affiliates every time a click is made on an ad on your affiliate's site that lands someone on your product page. You pay your affiliate whether a sale is made or not. If you went with pay-per-lead, you will have to pay for each lead that is sent your way.

Each pay model has its advantages and disadvantages. Most Internet marketers prefer to go with the pay-per-sale, as this is has the best ROI and payment system.

I'll cover each model below so you will gain an understanding of each one. Then you can make up your own mind as to which one you want to choose.

Pay-per-sale model

Of all payment models, this one is the most popular. You only have to pay your affiliates when they send a referral that buys your product. With this type of model, you are guaranteed a profit.

Pay-per-click model

With this model, you only pay your affiliates when someone clicks a link on the affiliate's website then lands on your product page. Typical fees paid out range from one cent to twenty-five cents, depending on the arrangement made, as well as the product and profit margin.

The problem with pay-per-click models is that you are not guaranteed a sale. In addition, the actual click may not be a customer, but could be a hacker or robot. In other words, you are taking a risk with each click.

Pay-per-lead model

With this model, you only pay your affiliates when they send a lead to you. For example, if someone visited your affiliate's website and filled out a form that led to you, this would be a lead that you would pay to your affiliate. The downside to this is it isn't a guaranteed sale, and the leads may not even be legit.

So there you have it. Affiliate programs can make you money whether you start one or sell products for others. This is actually one of the biggest ways to sell online. That is why it was placed first of all ways to make money online.

1.3. Affiliate Programs

I've talked about how can make money as an affiliate. Now you are going to learn about the various affiliate programs that you can get involved in. I will introduce a few popular ones here for you.

Advertising

If you have your own website, you can actually make money through advertising. For example, you can place a banner ad on your website. Every time someone comes to your site and clicks the banner, you make money. The people that sponsor the banner ad may choose to pay you per click, per impression, or per lead.

With the per-lead choice, you are only going to be paid when someone clicks the banner ad and ends up actually buying the product or taking some kind of action. This is why per-click or per-impression is the two best choices. It has been known that per-impression provides the highest conversion rate.

MySiteVideo

MySiteVideo allows webmasters to add video reviews to their website. They offer affiliates $50 commission for every sale generated. They also offer 10% to 2nd tier affiliates.

The Internet Millionaires Online Club is another great affiliate program. You can actually make automatic residual income by referring people to their site. Just promote a special affiliate link and when a person becomes a member, you get 50% commission every month.

To get started go to http://www.ziipa.com/tool/mysitevideo-com/

Market Health

Market Health started in 1998. Market Health is the world's largest integrated online marketing company in the health and beauty industry. They offer up to 60% or a flat CPA. They pay bi-weekly.

You can check them out by going to http://www.markethealth.com/.

Buy Sell Links

This program was created in 2004. BuySellLinks is one of the oldest Link Advertising websites on the Internet. BuySellLinks offers a reasonable commission structure of 10%-20%. They only offer a second-tier program. The commission is based on revenue. They pay monthly via PayPal.

You can learn more about them by going to http://www.buyselllinks.com/affiliate.php.

Staples

Staples is nearly everyone's office supply store. Millions of people buy products from Staples on a daily basis online and in the store. As long as you have a website, you can make money as an affiliate. You can make up to 5% of whatever the person you refer to buys.

If you wish to become an affiliate, just go to http://www.staples.com/sbd/content/about/affiliate/.

If you go to http://www.affiliateprograms.com/ you'll find a ton of affiliate programs you can get involved with offering great commissions.

1.4. Action Plan

To start your first action plan, let's go to the following URLs and do what you are instructed to do:

1. http://www.ziipa.com/tool/mysitevideo-com/
2. http://www.markethealth.com/
3. http://www.buyselllinks.com/affiliate.php
4. http://www.staples.com/sbd/content/about/affiliate/

1. To use Ziipa.com (http://www.ziipa.com/tool/mysitevideo-com/), click the green link at the top of the web page where it says "Create Your Dashboard."

After you click the green link, the following web page will pop up:

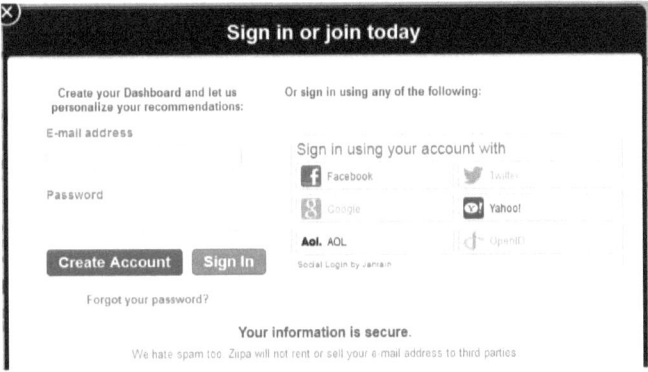

As you can see from the image, you can sign in using various methods.

2. To use MarketHealth (http://www.markethealth.com), go to the site, click the Affiliates link tab in the menu, and follow the instructions.

3. For BuySellLinks (http://www.buyselllinks.com/affiliate.php), go to the site and click "Join Affiliate

42

Program." Read the launch page. Then, when you are ready, click the small ">>click here to join" link at the bottom.

4. For Staples
(http://www.staples.com/sbd/content/about/affiliate/), go to the site and read the page. It explains everything.

After you have read everything on this page and you are satisfied with the terms and conditions, just click the link for the affiliate application link at the bottom of the page. The link will be in blue letters.

1.5. Your Notes

Use the space below to jot down anything you wish to remember as you proceed forward.

2.0. Use Google's AdSense

Are you familiar with Google AdSense? If not, this is a great method of making money. Google has a program that is directly tied to AdWords. What you can do is place selected ads on your website, and when someone sees the ad and clicks it, you make money from that click.

If you don't know what AdWords are, you need to get an understanding of this system first. Go to Google and type in a keyword about something of interest. For example, let's use the keyword "ipod touch."

Look at the image below and on the next page:

48

49

These are known as AdWord ads.

Okay, so how do these AdWords relate to AdSense? Here is how they interact. If you go to a website and see a bunch of ads that say "Ads by Google" or "Google Ads," these are AdSense ads. These are the ads you place on your website.

So how do you get these ads on your site? What you need to do first is go to https://accounts.google.com/ServiceLogin?service=adsense&rm=hide&nui=15&alwf=true&ltmpl=adsense&passive=true&continue=https://www.google.com/adsense/gaiaauth2&followup=https://www.google.com/adsense/gaiaauth2&hl=en_US.

Once you are there, you have to sign up. Just click the red box in the upper right hand corner. If you already have an account with Google (Gmail, AdWords, or Google+), you can select this method of signing in.

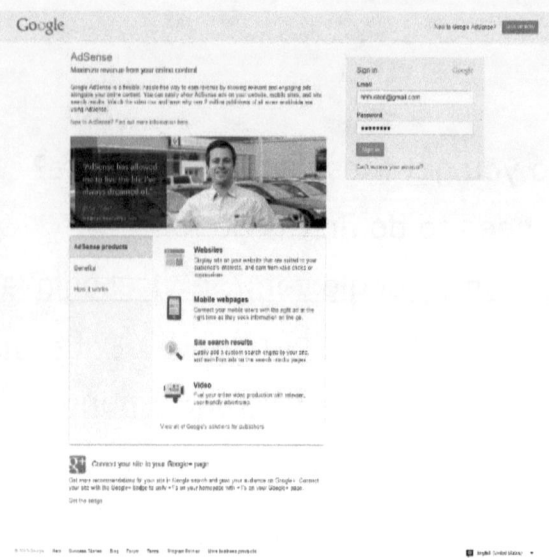

If you don't have any accounts at all with Google, you will need to select the second blue button.

If you choose to start a new account, just fill in the details provided on the web page. You will get an email a day or two later, letting you know if your account has been approved.

When you do get your email, and click the link, you will be taken to the main web page where you can begin working with AdSense. Once you have set up your account and decided on the type of AdSense ads you want to place on your website, just copy and paste the block of HTML, they provide and start showing the ads on your site.

There is one point to keep in mind regarding AdSense. They do have a large extensive advertiser base. This means you will have to choose from many different categories. The ads are targeted by geography. This will make it easier for you to choose a category.

Your biggest concern is to put the code they provide on your web page, wherever you want the ads to show. If you are not familiar with HTML, you may want to hire or ask someone to do this part for you. If you do know HTML, you are one step ahead.

53

Keep one thing in mind. The ads displayed are based on the theme of your web page and the keywords you have listed on the page. For instance, if you are selling information about Volkswagen Beetles, and you have a bunch of keywords on your page related to such cars, the ads will show something related to that car.

Guess what. Not only can you place ads on your site, you can also place a search box there was well. When you place a search box on a web page and someone uses it, you make money for that search.

When Google displays ads on your site, they review each ad to make sure it complies with their strict editorial guidelines. They use sensitive filters, your input, and a team of linguists, to make sure you only gets what is appropriate for your website.

If you know anything about web design, it would be a good idea to choose ad colors that allow the ads to blend in on your web page. This way the ads won't look awkward, and people won't think of them as ads.

You are not confined to placing the ads on one page. You can place the code on every page if you like. When you have the ads showing on more than one page, you stand a greater chance of making more money.

2.1. Action Plan

To get started, go to https://accounts.google.com/ServiceLoginAuth?continue=https%3A%2F%2Fwww.google.com%2Fadsense%2Fgaiaauth2&followup=https%3A%2F%2Fwww.google.com%2Fadsense%2Fgaiaauth2&service=adsense&nui=15&rm=hide&ltmpl=adsense&hl=en_US&alwf=true and sign up. It takes less than five minutes. After you have filled out the application and submitted it, you will need to wait till you get the confirmation email.

When you get the confirmation email, proceed to go through the AdSense system and set up the ads that will be placed on your website. You will be presented with channels. Pick the channels you believe matches closest the channels your website belongs in. Google will do everything possible to match the ads they show on your web pages to this channel, instead of showing ads randomly.

2.2. Your Notes

At this time, if you have any comments or suggestions, or just want to remember your username and password, use this space to make notes. You may also want to write down what your website theme is so you'll have a better idea of which channels to pick.

3.0. Write and Sell E-books

Do you consider yourself a writer? Do you have many ideas floating around in your head that are anxious to come out? You don't have to be an expert wordsmith. As long as people can understand what you say and learn from it, that is what's important.

E-book sales surpassed paperback and hardcover sales by a big margin. Over $359 billion dollars was spent last year on e-books. Writing and selling e-books is a very profitable business.

The great part about writing e-books is that once you have completed the e-book, when you sell it, the amount you make is pure profit. This is because you don't have to work with any middle man.

Do you have something interesting you can write? I know when I think of something, I can't wait to write it. If you are unsure what to write about, you can always do a search online and find out what the latest trend is. Obviously, information is the biggest winner. Self-help, self-development, and how-to topics are most in demand. If you can write in one of these areas, you can make a lot of money.

For example, if you knew how to lose 20lbs in a week, and you wrote "How to Take Off 20lbs in a Week and Keep It Off," you would be surprised by how many people would buy it, especially those who are in the process of losing weight, or want to learn how to lose weight.

If you are interested in writing an e-book, the steps you can take to help you do that include:

1. Decide what the e-book will be about. What is the purpose for the e-book? Here

are some topics you may want to consider: Internet marketing, health, fitness, or IT. As long as you can teach something that people don't know or can put a different spin on it, you will succeed in providing a very successful e-book.

2. Understand your target market. Do you know your target market? If you know your target market, do you know what their biggest concerns, worries, or problems are? In order to sell what you write, you have to appeal to your target market. If you don't have a target market, you must find one first. Let's say you have no idea of your target market. In this case, make a list of your passions and interests. Once you have your passions and interests down, place the word "how" in front of them. Now, you can come up with a ton of ideas to write about that will sell to people.

3. Once you have your passions and interests down, it is time to find out if there's a market for what you have written down. To research this, you need to use a keyword tool. When using the keyword tool, type in the word of interest along with the word "how" and see what comes up. You will be surprised at the keyword phrases that appear. This is how you can find what people are looking for. You can also go to groups and social sites and find out what the biggest problems or complaints are.

4. When you know what people want or need, write an e-book to help. You don't have to write that many pages. Many e-books are between 30 and 50 pages. The page count will depend on the subject matter and/or how much you know about the subject. As you write, keep your sentences sharp and focused. Do not veer off onto a tangent. Avoid writing fluff. You

61

will lose your readers that way. The best way to write is by using the KISS method (keep it simple stupid). Don't use fancy words. You just want the material to be clear and concise.

7. Complete a spell and grammar check. When you have completed writing, go back and re-read what you wrote. Nine times out of ten, you will end up revising the material. This is why it is important to do a spell and grammar check after finishing the e-book.

8. Convert the file into a PDF document. Once you have confirmed the document is 100% accurate, now you can use the convert command in Word to change the document to PDF format. Save the file in DOC format first, in case you have to go back and edit the book. When you are ready to convert to PDF, click File and Click Save

As. Then in the "Save as type" field, choose PDF.

9. Upload the PDF version of your e-book to your web host's server. This is the same place where your other web files are located. Make sure to put a link to it on the web page where you plan to sell it.

Do you have an idea that people may be interested in learn or reading about? If you do, why sit around with it in your head. Instead, write it out and let people read it. That way you stand a chance at helping others, while making good money to boot.

3.1. Action Plan

For this activity, there are two steps involved.

Step one:

Write down all your passions and interests.
You can use the free space under Your
Notes below to record them.

Step two:

Go to one of these sites:

1. https://freekeywords.wordtracker.com/
2. https://adwords.google.com/o/Targeting/Explorer? c=1000000000& u=1000000000&ideaRequestType=KEYWORD IDEAS
3. http://www.wordstream.com/keywords
4. http://www.keyworddiscovery.com/search.html

The choice of keyword tool is up to you. I
gave you a list of the free ones. Look at
each one and determine for yourself the
tool that you feel most comfortable with.

Look up the passions and interests you have written down and see what keywords you come up with.

3.2. Your Notes

If you wish, you can use this space to write down all the passions and interests you have. The more you list, the greater the chance you will find a niche that is right for you. Keep in mind you are writing and selling e-books. As such, use this space to keep track of what you are doing with your ideas and with your e-book writing.

4.0. Sell Products on EBay

If you have an account with eBay.com, you can make money auctioning your stuff. There are various ways for you to make money with eBay. In order to sell on eBay, you need to how the system works. In addition, you have to know what products are sold the most.

The first thing you need to do is set up an account, unless you already have one. Once you have an account and log on to eBay, you will notice the front page contains a list of what is hot for the day. Use this to tell what is being sold the most. When you have something that fits within this host list, you stand a better chance of selling your stuff.

When you set up an auction, it can be listed as either an auction or Buy It Now. You can request a starting bid at the price you want.

67

Once you set up your auction, you can specify the number of days for the auction to be active. After the auction has concluded, and you didn't sell the item, you can have the item listed again for free.

You can also take advantage of eBay's store feature. If you have many items, you can create a store on eBay and set it up so those who want to place bids can go to your store and bid on whatever you have. Alternatively, if you have it set up, you can request a fixed price for your items.

There are many people that use eBay to sell their items. Just go to eBay.com now and look at some categories. Look around. See what the bids are like. With some items, you may see more than one bid.

If you have items that may be antique or historical, take a look at this category and see if there are any items that come close to yours. This way you will see if there are any bids for those items or not. If you do your homework, you'll be able to tell what is going to sell on eBay and what won't.

There are actually people making money on eBay on a full-time basis. Once you know how to work the system, you'll be able to make money on eBay as well.

4.1. Action Plan

For this activity, go to www.ebay.com and sign up. Just click the register button at the top of the page. When you click register, you will be required to fill in your name and email. You will have to create a user ID and a password. Once you click Submit, you will receive an email for confirmation. After you confirm your email, your account will be active.

Create an auction for anything in your home. Look in your closet, attic, or shed and find something you no longer want but that someone else may like. Once you find something, create your auction and allow it to run about 7 days. This should be enough time. After the 7 days have been completed, you will know whether you have sold anything or not.

4.2. Your Notes

If you like, you can write your username and password down in the space below. This way you can remember it. You can also use the space to record anything else you desire. Perhaps notes on the item you are selling, along with your price, opening bid, and closing bid. Maybe a list of other items you might want to sell.

5.0. Sell Products on Your Website

If you have a website, why not use it to sell products. You already know you can sell e-books. However, you aren't confined to just selling e-books. If there is a market for it, you can sell just about anything.

If you want to sell products on your website, you first have to create one. If you already have a website, evaluate the way it looks. You may have to make some changes to conform to what you are selling. If you don't have a website set up, it is time to consider it.

When creating your website, you need a picture of the product you are selling, this way people can see what your product is visually. The next step is to place copy on the site that will help sell the product. The last thing you need, and the important one, is an order page. This is where you will send people to order your product from the product listing page.

If you aren't sure what to sell on your website, here is a list of products that are in demand:

1. E-books
2. Flowers
3. Video games
4. Videos
5. Audios
6. Memberships
7. Poker
8. Pornography

If you are going to set up a website to sell products, keep in mind that you want to sell only what people want. If you put up products that people don't want or care about, you won't make any sales. You have to know what people are looking for. Make sure there is a demand for the product. As long as there is a demand, you will make money.

If you are very new to the online world, and want to sell products on your website, here are the steps you will need to take:

- Create a domain. Pick a name that highlights what your product is about. When you pick the right name and people see it, they will know right away, what the site is about.
- After you create your domain name, register it. You can go to a registrar like GoDaddy.com and register for only about $12.77 per domain name.
- After you register your domain name, you will need to find a web hosting company to take care of your website when you upload your files. If you do

not have one, use Google to find one. GoDaddy offers a very reasonable hosting package. In fact, with every new domain created, you get free web hosting.

- The next step is to create your web pages. If you know HTML, you can use Notepad to create the pages. If you have no clue about HTML, you will need a web design editor like Dreamweaver or Coffee Cup. On the other hand, if you'd rather, there are free online HTML editors you can use. They are limited, but at least you can have your website up and operational quickly. The direction you go with your web design will depend on how much experience you have in HTML coding and creating web pages.

- After you have chosen an HTML editor or website creator, it is time to build your web pages. Start by giving your web page a title. This is the first thing people will see. Under or over the top of the title you can place an image of your product. It can be your logo, a banner, or something visual.

- Create an order page so your customers will be able to order from you, with a shopping cart system in place to make ordering easy.
- After you have created your web page, upload it to your web host's server. FTP is the most often used method of uploading files. The problem with this is that you will need a program that provides you access to your web host's server. You normally will need a username and password for this.

The most often used software for

uploading is FileZilla. You will need to contact your web hosting technical support for help setting up the file upload software, as that goes beyond the scope of this e-book.

After you have uploaded all your files, the next step is to promote your website. Once your site goes live, Google will come and index it. However, don't depend on Google. You have to promote your site yourself. You can do this a number of ways. For example, you can join social media sites and mention your site in your posts and comments.

5.1. Action Plan

Putting this into action involves four steps.

Step one:

Write down what you would like to sell on your website. List as many products you can think of. You can use the Your Notes section of this chapter to do this. As you make the list, keep in mind the reason for writing things down. What you are looking for is something that is tangible, something you can sell easily from your website. Make sure the product you have selected is something you have an interest in or you may drop it from boredom or lack of interest eventually.

After you have listed all the products, you would like to sell, pick one to start with. This one should be the most popular one, so you can make money fast with it. If you have a website set up, alter it to accommodate the product you selected. If you have no website or domain selected, this is the time to find one that comes close to matching the kind of product you have selected. As such, proceed to step two.

Step two:

Go to www.godaddy.com and find a domain that will correspond to the product you decided you want to sell on your site. Once you find the domain, register it.

Step three:

Review and choose which web hosting company you will go with. You can either go with GoDaddy for now, or go to Google and search Web Hosting.

Step four:

After you have chosen your web hosting company, build your website. It doesn't have to be huge. Just create a landing page, along with an order page, for starters. You can always add onto it later.

5.2. Your Notes

Use this space to write down the list of products you would like to sell on your website. You can also use this area to record the domain you selected so you can remember it or to write down whatever else you think of and want to remember as you work the above steps.

6.0. Buy an Internet Business

If you currently don't own your own online business, you can always buy one from someone else. By buying an Internet business, you can avoid the headaches of having to create one from scratch. This makes the process of owning and running a business much easier.

If you are an entrepreneur type, maybe this is a great time to get involved in a business. There are plenty of opportunities online. Just be careful, as some are scams, while others will be legit.

Some of these opportunities claim they will give you a website for free. Just sign up. After you have signed up, you will get a website right away. The problem with this is that many other people have done the same thing, so there are probably thousands of people, using the same template website to sell the same thing.

Some opportunities are legit. They may be advertised on a legit advertising site. You purchase the site from the owner, and you become the new owner. With this kind of opportunity, you get the website, domain name, and hosting company. You still have to do your own promoting.

Before you think about buying an Internet business, you should consider a number of factors. Above all, you must be sure the business is legit. There are steps you can take to verify that the business you want to invest in is legit:

1. Why is it for sale? Is the owner going under financially? Is the site getting enough traffic? Is the owner doing enough to promote the site? What

about income? Is the site actually making money?

2. Ask what is included in the asking price. You don't want to hand your money over until you know for sure what is behind the sale of the site. Why is the owner selling the business for the price he's asking? What are you getting for the money you are spending on that business?

3. Do your homework. Investigate the owner and the business thoroughly. Check out the sites stats before you make any kind of move. By checking the stats, you will know exactly how much traffic you will be getting.

4. Check the name of the site with a domain appraiser to determine what the site is actually worth. For example, if the owner is asking $5000 for the site, and the appraiser said the

site was only worth $650, you know the owner is either greedy or full of himself. If the appraised value is higher than $5000, and the owner is asking for about $1000, you will be getting the site at a bargain price.

5. Before you give him the money, negotiate. Give him an offer lower than his asking price, but not too low. See what he says. If he counters your offer with a bigger offer, you can either back away, or counter his counter-offer. When you have agreed to the final price, make sure it isn't higher than the appraised value or you'll pay too much.

6. When you and the owner agree to terms, have everything written down so both of you are protected in case of some legal entanglement.

If you are serious about buying a business online, do your research first. Understand what you are getting into. Go for an Internet business where the products are in big demand. This is how you can make a lot of money. Buying a business online can be a lucrative business if you find one that you like, that interests you, and that you can afford to buy. Just be careful out there. There are sharks in the water. Make sure you aren't bitten.

6.1. Action Plan

To put this into action, go to www.ebay.com and look at the business and industrial section. In the Browse By menu, select Businesses & Websites for Sale. Under Categories, take a look at Internet Businesses & Websites. Look at all the items and see if there are any you might be interested in purchasing.

You can also go to
http://www.bizbuysell.com/internet-
companies-for-sale/ and take a look at what
is available.

6.2. Your Notes

Write down a list of websites you find
interesting at the above sites. Write down
each site including a review of the site and
its price. Then evaluate each site to
determine which one you think is the best
fit for you and go for that one.

7.0. Working as a Freelancer

One great way to make money online is by being a freelancer. If you like your independence, and don't mind the seclusion that working for yourself can bring, then you may be successful as a freelancer. As a freelancer, you get to choose the projects work on and decide how much money you want to make.

Do you know that with the popularity of the Internet, there are many people who work online? These freelancers create a website and promote their services by way of social media sites, article marketing, video marketing, and many other marketing venues.

If you are new to freelancing, this is what you will need to do as well. The only way to get people interested in your services is by creating a web presence. You can start out by creating a well thought out website that features your services, whatever they may be. If you specialize in a certain kind of service, emphasize that.

If you are the type that likes to work on your own, then it is time for you to get started. Here are some tips you can use to help you get started as a freelancer:

1. Know what you want to do. Think about your skills, as well as talents, and what you bring to the table. Write these down. This list will help you determine what you are can do as a freelancer.

2. Do a search for freelance jobs that match your skills and experience. If your choice of job is as a writer, look for freelance writing websites. If you'd

rather be an accountant, look for those websites.

3. Do your homework. Find out what people in the profession you wish to engage in are making. This will be the price point you want to go with. Make sure you know what to charge because, if you don't and someone comes along asking for it, you might lose a customer.

4. Take on only the projects that fit your skills and talents. The last thing you need is to look bad with your client. You'll get a bad reputation if you start taking jobs you can't handle just because you need the money.

5. There will be some measure of risk. For example, there may be a slow paying client. On the other hand, there could be a bad seed. He may contract you for work, but never pay

you. Before starting a project, always get everything in writing, and request a deposit up front. This way you will know the client is serious about what they want, and you can trust that they will pay you the balance they owe.

6. Once you have made your decision as to what project to take on, send the client a disclosure agreement (if required), and a contract for them to sign. Always ask for a deposit up front. Even if it is small, at least by submitting a deposit, you know the client is serious about working with you.

7. Take steps to work on the project, communicating with the client every so often to let him/her know your progress.

8. When you have completed the project, it is time to submit your final invoice for payment.

You can make a great deal of money as a freelancer. Using the Internet increases your chances of making good money. However, there are risks. Sometimes there will be plenty of money, and other times there won't be anything. It comes and goes. The great part about freelancing is you control your own hours and income.

7.1. Websites for Freelancers

If you are new to freelancing, especially as a writer, there are websites you can go to for work. These sites are listed below:

Elance.com (www.elance.com)

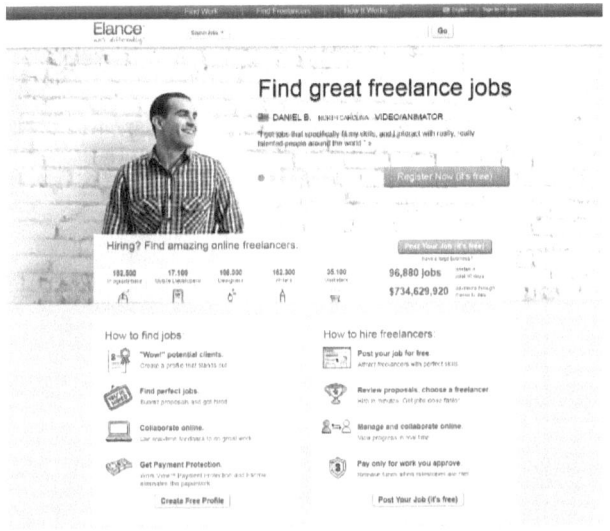

With Elance, you can sign up as a freelancer and begin applying for projects right away. It is just a matter of signing up, creating a profile, and then providing a way to accept money. Once you do that, you are on your way to making money. Elance currently has well over 100,000 service providers and that list is growing every day. Some people have been known to make up to $150,000 a year on Elance.

Guru.com (www.guru.com)

Guru is another site that allows writers to make money. Just like Elance, you have to sign up. Signing up is self-explanatory. Once you sign up, you can begin to look for projects right away. Before looking for projects, make sure to fill out the category listing, this way Guru will know what areas of interest you like. They need to know this because when you set up searches to have them emailed to you, they want to know exactly what areas of writing you do so they can send the right leads.

ODesk (www.odesk.com)

ODesk is similar to Elance and Guru as it is a site where you can find work. You sign up first and then create a profile. The profile is extensive. Once you have filled in your profile, the site encourages you to upload a photo of yourself and to take tests to show your skillset. The tests are free.

The jobs are either pay-per-hour or a fixed-project price. When you do the per-hour jobs, you get higher ranking on ODesk.

7.2. Action Plan

Putting this into action takes two steps.

Step one:

Using the Your Notes section or a separate piece of paper, write down the type of services you have done in the past and can offer to people. These services can be online or offline. If you are looking to aim your services for the online world, you need to circle those services that you can offer and perform online.

For example, if you are a videographer, you can set up a website where you can record videos for clients that they can upload online. Whatever service you choose, you need to adapt it to the online world, so look for services you can deploy online.

Step two:

Go to Elance.com, Guru.com, Odesk.com, freelancewriting.com, vWorker, Freelancer.com, 99designs, crowdSPRING, and Fiverr. Read over their terms and conditions. Rate each one and determine the site or sites you wish to work with. Once you have determined what site or sites to work with, register with them and start applying for jobs.

You may find that you won't win projects from these sites immediately. This is when you will need patience. Eventually, if you put in enough bids, you will begin getting work.

7.3. Your Notes

Use this area to include your thoughts from step one of Action Plan above.

8.0. Get Paid to Programs

You may not realize this, but there are ways of making money on the Internet that don't require selling any of your own products. This involves participating in "get paid to" programs. In other words, you are paid to do something.

If you go online and do a search, you will find there are many "get paid to" programs available. For example, there are programs that pay you to read emails. They pay you so much per email you respond to.

The reason companies are willing to pay you to read emails is because they are so busy with promoting their products or services that they don't have the time to respond to emails from customers. They may hire a certain number of customer service reps to help out, but even those few may not be able to handle the case load. They hire a freelancer like you to answer emails for them.

Other "get paid to" programs include being paid to click and surf the Internet, being paid to take surveys, or being paid to shop online. There are many such programs you can get involved in. Just be careful and read the fine-print.

Although there are many legit "get paid to" programs, there are also scams. Read the fine print. Don't get involved in something just because the company sponsoring the program says you can make a ton of money. Take your time and don't pay a dime. If these are legit programs, you won't have to pay any amount to join. Just sign up and be paid when you do the work.

The primary way for you to be paid through these programs is by performing some kind of action. Many companies have cookies that they install on your computer. These cookies record your every movement and report these movements back to the site where you signed up for the program.

How can you get involved in such "get paid to" programs? Here are some programs you can find online and how you can get involved:

1. Get paid to read emails: Once you sign up with the company, they will send you emails or they will have you log into their system remotely. Once you are connected, they will tell you what emails to answer. Most likely, they will sort them out and place them in a folder for you to access.

   Your job is to simply read and respond. When you respond to the email, your response is recorded and you are paid for that response. Some of these companies even pay per referral to help you make even more money. Here is one example of such a site: http://www.emailcashpro.com/.

2. Get paid to click: After you sign up, you will have various options to make money. Just go to a particular website, sign up, and follow their instructions. When you click an ad or perform an event, you are paid. Here is an example of such a site: http://www.clixsense.com/.

3. Get paid to surf: There are many ways to make money surfing the Internet. In order to understand how this works, you will need to go to a site that specializes in offering this kind of program. Basically, you fill out some kind of information so the

company can keep track of your every move. As you move around the Internet, and you click on links, you are paid a small amount of money for each click you perform.

Here is a website that lists several surfing programs. Take a look and see which one works better for you: http://www.itsvery.net/paidtosurf.html#surf.

4. Get paid to surveys: This is a big the most often sought after option. The catch to this is you have to like filling out surveys. You can make a lot of money doing it though. Here is a website that offers such a program: http://www.bigspot.com/?c=BigSpot.

5. Get paid to advertise: With this program, you are promoting someone else's website or products in return to

being paid. Here is a site that features such a program: http://zeekrewardsnews.com/you-get-paid-to-advertise/.

These are programs where you can make money. You won't get rich working them, but at least you'll be able to make some kind of income from it.

8.1. Action Plan

To put this into action, just go to each one of the websites as listed below and sign up to work with them. Make sure to read the fine print first. You want to make sure you know what you are getting into.

1. http://www.emailcashpro.com/

2. http://www.clixsense.com/

3.
http://www.itsvery.net/paidtosurf.html#surf

4. http://www.bigspot.com/?c=BigSpot

5. http://zeekrewardsnews.com/you-get-paid-to-advertise/

While you are at it, go to Google or another search engine, and type in "Get paid to" in the search field. When the search results page comes up, make note of the programs that are available.

8.2. Your Notes

Use this space freely to track websites or other information you need to implement this section.

9.0. Flipping Websites and Domains

In this section, you will learn how to make money flipping websites and domains. Let's start with websites.

Websites

If you like designing websites, you may like doing this as a way to make money online. Any time you buy and sell a business for profit, it puts money in your pocket. Who doesn't want to make a profit? The Internet makes making money even easier.

If you have the money to go for a website, why not purchase one. As long as you have the knowledge to fix it up and make it perform better, why not. Think about the ROI you would get when you re-sell it.

Buying a website to flip is not really that costly. A website can cost a few dollars to a few hundred dollars. The great part about buying an existing website is that you don't have to spend a lot of time or money trying to get traffic to the site. That has already been taken care of. In addition, you don't have to wait for the site to be indexed. That has also been taken care of.

So how do you go about buying and flipping a website? This can be a risky endeavor if you don't know what you are doing. The best way to make money flipping a site is to find one that is not performing well, buy it, and fix it so it performs well. Then sell it for double the price you paid, if possible.

The best site is one that sells a product that is in good demand. For example, this site could be one that is just starting out but the current owner doesn't have the marketing skills or the time to deal with it. Instead of trying to fix the problem, the owner would rather sell it.

When you buy a website to flip it, your main concern is to quickly implement the change, fix whatever needs to be fixed, tweak the site a bit, and then when you have the site performing well, sell it for double the price you paid for it. In order to be successful with website buying and flipping, you must realize that the Internet is the fastest industry when it comes to competition.

You have to stay current with what is happening on the Internet, so you will know what products are hot. You won't want to buy into a site that doesn't have a hot product. Otherwise, you may be stuck with a site you can't unload.

One site that would be a goldmine for you is a site with a massive forum that is filled with a nice target niche audience. Amateurs usually create such a site. They have no idea how to monetize it.

The bandwidth has probably gotten so out of control, they don't want to pay the extra money for the bandwidth. Instead of dealing with the website and the costs of it, they'd rather sell it. With this type of site, you just have to monetize it by placing ads on the site, and then sell it for a good price.

Another site you may want to consider buying is a popular domain name. If you have the money for it, purchase a popular domain name and then flip it quickly. You can sell it for a much higher price.

Where do you go to purchase websites for sale? You can start here: http://www.entrepreneurs-journey.com/266/how-to-sell-a-website-how-much-is-your-website-worth/.

110

Besides the above website, you can use Google to find websites operating in an industry you feel confident about. Don't look for the big sites or the sites on the first few pages of search results, unless you can clearly see they have potential. They may be in an industry with low to no competition. Identify sites that have potential, not those that are already optimized or poor and not doing anything.

When you are ready to buy a website, take time to monitor and research it. Check for any backlinks to the site. Investigate the site's history. You can do this by going to the Wayback Machine.

Check to see if the site has forums, chatrooms, blog posts, comments, helpdesk, etc. Make sure to check the site design, the structure of the links, headings, titles, and keyword density. Check the site statistics if they are available. You can check this by going to Alexa.

After you have done your homework, contact the owner and strike up a deal. You should be able to find the owner's email address on the site. If you can't, go to WhoIs database where you will find the email address for the person that registered the domain.

When you get in touch with the owner, introduce yourself and let him know you like his site and then see how much interest the owner has in his website. Get a feel for how the owner feels about his site. Soon after, let him know you are interested in making a purchase. Let him know the price you are willing to pay. Don't forget to negotiate. The owner normally won't accept your first offer.

If the owner agrees to your terms, you will have to perform the following:

- Log into his account, unless he prefers to do this himself, and have the domain set up to transfer to your register. Depending on the registrar of the account, the transfer process may be easy or hard.
- Get a contract made up outlining the deal and have all parties sign and date it. Make sure to include a clause that will keep the previous owner from starting up a competing site immediately after the sale.
- If there is any download list, make sure to download it, as you will now be the owner of it.
- Ask the previous owner to be available for a few weeks after the sale to answer any questions that may arise when you start using the site.

Flipping a site can be very lucrative, if you plan it well. Do your homework first. You'll be glad you did.

Domains

Flipping domain names is another way to make money online. This system works by researching and finding good names for domains. People have problems. Creating a domain that has a keyword in it that matches one of the keywords that is being used for searching will cause that domain to be not only popular but also to rank higher in search results.

Search for keywords using a keyword tool. Find out what people need. You can start with your passions or interests and proceed from there. Once you understand what people are looking for, you can then create a bunch of names for domains.

After you have created the domain names, go to a register of domains like GoDaddy.com and see if they have a special for bulk domain registration. If they don't, you may have to pay for each one individually. Depending how many domains you register, this could cost you up to $12 per domain.

Once you have registered your domains, give the register some time to set your registration so the domains belong to you. Once you are declared the owner, you can then put the domains up for sale. When you do put the domains up for sale, you can charge whatever you want.

The best way to find out what the best price is for your domains is to get your domains appraised by a domain appraisal service. At that time, you'll be able to tell the value of your domains and the amount you can sell them for. It is important to know the appraised value, as this is the lowest price you will be able to accept.

For instance, let's say your domain is appraised at $2500. This is the minimum that you will accept when you sell the domain. If you go below that amount, you will be too low. Flipping domains will work as long as you go for domains that are big winners and can provide you with the big bucks.

9.1. Action Plan

For this activity, start your search by going to http://www.entrepreneurs-journey.com/266/how-to-sell-a-website-how-much-is-your-website-worth/. Look for sites that are for sale and check them out.

9.2. Your Notes

Record the sites you like from the above search and make notes on what you like about each site, this way you can decide whether to invest in the site or not.

10.0. Answering Questions

Do you know you can make money by answering questions? You'd be surprised just how many people will pay you to answer their questions. If people are desperate enough, they will pay good money to get the information they desire. There are even websites that were created, backed by experts that answer questions of visitors for a certain fee.

If you are an expert with some subject, why not take advantage of this type of program and make money from it. The amount of money you can get per question will depend on the question, topic, and the one paying. It is a great way to make money online in your spare time.

Below are some of the websites where you can sign up and offer yourself as a paying expert.

Weegy.com

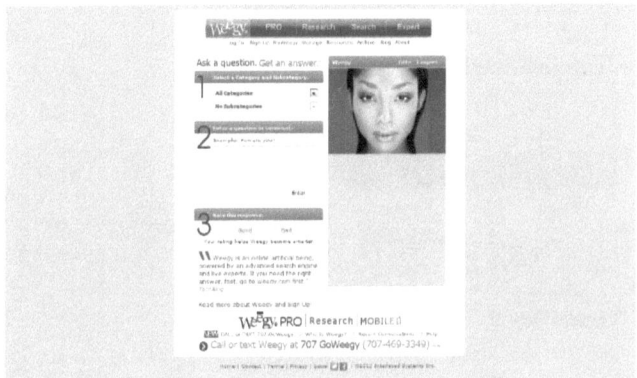

Weegy is an artificial intelligence system. It takes a question and supplies answers to the user. The questions are sent by text message, called in, or entered by an online portal. If the automatic system cannot answer the question, an expert is on standby to answer that question. For each question answered, the expert receives cash by way of PayPal.

Justanswer.com

If you are an expert in an industry and can prove it, you can make a good deal of money by signing up at Justanswer.com. The site gets at least a thousand hits or more a day. The sign up process is easy.

Just sign up and let them know what industry or field you are an expert in and they will set you up with an account. Soon after, people will begin connecting with you.

If you write a really powerful profile, you will be getting many responses. Once the person picks you, provide as detailed an answer as you can. If they like your response, they will select it and you are paid.

You don't have to wait for a response. If you are aggressive, you can find all unanswered questions in a pool and answer them. In this way, you can get a following and make a ton of money as well.

ChaCha.com

Chacha allows you to make money as an online guide. An online guide is someone who answers questions. It's like a search engine in a way, except it is run by humans. In other words, you get a live person to help you. The answer chosen can be sent by computer or by phone.

It is a great way for you to make steady income. Just go there and sign up as a guide. You'll begin getting business pretty quickly.

10.1. Action Plan

For this activity, go to each of the sites listed below and register. Once you have done that, start answering questions.

http://www.weegy.com/?r=50EAFC63

http://becomeaguide.chacha.com/

http://www.justanswer.com/

10.2. Your Notes

Use this space to jot down your username and password for each site and/or other notes, if you wish.

11.0. Video Creator

If you have a video camera or camcorder, you can make money online. The only thing more you need is a video editing program. Start by creating a video of yourself or your business, and upload it to video sites.

In the video, explain what your service is and how you go about it. State what type of videos you work with. At the end of your video, in big letters, post your website URL, so people know where to go to learn more about your video services.

When your video is finished, place the video on your own website, right on the front page. You can also upload the video to YouTube if you like, and then let people know how to view it.

Besides YouTube.com, you can also upload your video to sites like Ulinkx.com,

Break.com, and so on. Here is an actual list of the websites, where you can upload your video:

1. **YouTube-** Upload your video to YouTube and point people to the link so they can view it. This is a great way to get a lot of exposure. Your message can go viral. When one person views your video, they can forward it to someone else, and so on.

2. **Break.com-** The difference between this site and other video sites is that if your video appears on the front page, you can earn as much as $2,000.

3. **Lulu.com-**Lulu.com has become very popular in recent years. When you publish your videos, you can earn money when people view them.

4. **Blip.tv-** Blip.tv provides many ways for you to make money with your videos.

5. **Vuze.com-** Vuze is a different animal. They allow you to create videos with ads or without them.

When you advertise yourself as a video creator, you will gain a lot of exposure, simply by uploading your videos so others can see them. It's a great way to promote yourself quickly.

Before long, you'll be getting a lot of business. You'll be booking projects well in advance, as long as you have a great camcorder that records top-quality videos. What is even more impressive is that if you show your potential clients that you can stream videos so they appear online, that will be even more impressive as an incentive to hire you.

11.1. Action Plan

For this activity, go to each of the sites listed below and register. Once you have done that, begin creating videos and uploading them.

1. YouTube- http://www.youtube.com/

2. Break.com- http://www.break.com/

3. Lulu.com- www.lulu.com

4. Blip.tv- http://www.blip.tv/

5. Vuze.com- http://www.vuze.com/

11.2. Your Notes

As you visit the sites above, why not write down your login information so you won't forget it. You can also write down key ideas of videos you wish to create to demonstrate your services.

12.0. Make Money from Blogging

If you like blogging, or have your own blog, you can make money from it. In fact, blogging has caught fire in recent years and has proven to be the biggest money maker around.

You may think that blogging consists of mainly personal blogs, but that isn't the case. Business people put up blogs. Entrepreneurs are blogging about their work or industry. You may be surprised at who blogs today.

Blogging has become more than just a place to discuss personal issues or important business matters. People use blogs to make money as well. If you go to a blog site, you may see a place on the blog with "Ads by

Google" or "Google Ads." These are actually referred to as Google AdSense ads.

AdSense ads are based on ads that advertisers created in AdWords. AdWords is a pay-per-click system. When you bid on a keyword or two and write ads based on those keywords, those ads show up in search results on the right hand side of the search results page. Every time someone clicks the ad, the advertiser has to pay for that click.

This is how pay-per-click works. Now how does that work in relation to AdSense? When you go to Google AdSense and sign up, you are agreeing with Google that you want to display one or a group of ads on your web page. The ads that you agree to place on your web page are ads created in AdWords. This is why AdWords and AdSense work together.

131

Even though the program is called AdSense, when you place a cluster of ads from Google on your web page, you are in fact placing ads that were created using the AdWords platform. Every time someone visits your site and clicks one of the ads, you just made the same amount of money that the advertiser paid.

Google pays you for the click because, when Google makes money from the advertiser for clicks in search results, they take that money and pay you, as an incentive for you to help show the advertiser's ads.

If you want to take advantage of this free program to make money from your blog, just sign up at this signup page: AdSense program.

If you want to check out other advertising programs, here is a list of them below:

BidVertiser (http://www.bidvertiser.com/)

If you want to do more advertising then just with AdSense, you can use BidVertiser. AdSense pays money when an account reaches $100. However, BidVertiser pays when the account reaches $10.

Clicksor (http://www.clicksor.com/)

If you want to look at many different types of ads, you can take a look at Clicksor. You can use a text banner ad just like in AdSense. You can also use inline text ads as well.

These are great places where you can sign up to have ads placed on your site. By monetizing your blog, you can make money when people visit it.

You can also make money from your blog by advertising your own product. If you use

WordPress, you can install a widget that will allow you to advertise whatever you like. What better way to entice your blog visitors than to place a link to your product on your blog. People will see it. If the ad is convincing enough, they will click the link and order your product.

There are other ways you can make money besides what I mentioned above. You can also join programs that will help you earn money. Here are some of those programs:

- BlogAds.com: They list over 3500 blogs. In order to be listed you need to have at least 1,000 page views (aka hits) per day or more on your blog.
- Smorty.com: You can be paid by accepting ad campaigns to write about and placing those postings on your blog. When someone clicks a

product that is related to a Smorty.com post on your blog, you earn a commission.

- PayPerPost.com: With this, advertisers give you an opportunity to write about their products on your blog. If the post you provide is approved, you are paid.

Keep the above sites in mind. If you follow the steps, you will see just how easy making money from your blog will be.

12.1. Action Plan

For this activity, go to each of the sites listed below and register. Then begin making money from your blog.

BidVertiser (http://www.bidvertiser.com/)

Clicksor (http://www.clicksor.com/)

BlogAds.com (http://www.blogads.com)

Smorty.com (http://www.smorty.com)

PayPerPost.com (http://www.smorty.com)

12.2. Your Notes

There are a number of other ways for you to make money from your blog besides those listed above. Why not go to Google and find other ways to make money? Write your ideas in the space below and then act on them. The more ideas you come up with and implement, the more money you can make from your blog.

13.0. Make Money with Amazon

Are you a member of Amazon? If so, do you buy things from them occasionally? Do you know that you can also sell things on Amazon and receive payment for it? There are many stores and individuals selling their products on Amazon. When you sign up, you can create a store front where you can advertise all your products for people to view and buy.

Have you ever visited Amazon, and took a look at a product, only to see that the product is also sold through other vendors. You will see under the actual product, places where the product is also available.

Price: **$9.97** *Prime*
Special Offers Available

In Stock.
Ships from and sold by **Amazon.com**. Gift-wrap available.

10 new from $8.80   **1 used** from $8.00

Formats	Amazon Price	New from	Used from
Kindle Edition	$2.99	--	--
Paperback	$9.97 *Prime*	$8.80	$8.00

If you look at the image above, take a look under "In Stock." You will see "10 new" and "1 used." These are store owners or vendors selling this item as well. Some vendors sell their item for more and others sell theirs for less.

The main point here is that if you sign up to sell products on Amazon, you can make a ton of money. That is a guarantee. Many people sell their items on Amazon every day. You just need to have products to sell.

If you can do that, you are on your way to making a lot of money on Amazon.

Keep in mind one thing. If you sell books, you won't make much. As you know, most books are now on Kindle. These books are rarely sold over $10. You would need to sell a ton of these Kindle books a day to make good money.

Amazon is not just about selling books. They sell many types of items as well. You just have to know what you want to sell and how much you want to sell it for. To learn more about how to sell at Amazon, click here:

http://www.amazon.com/gp/help/customer/display.html/ref=hp_sn_sell?nodeId=1161232.

Amazon makes the process easy. When you are all set up, place a couple of items on the system, and see how quickly it sells.

Amazon provides you more ways to sell than just by listing your items. They have many programs available to allow you to make money with them.

Go to http://www.amazon.com/gp/seller-account/mm-landing.html to learn about other ways of making money with Amazon. Amazon wants to help you make money. By using one or all of the programs you see at the above site, you'll soon see just how much money you can make.

13.1. Action Plan

For this activity, go to http://www.amazon.com/gp/seller-account/mm-landing.html and check out each offer. There are five different ways for you to make money with Amazon.

These are:

- Selling on Amazon
- Fulfillment by Amazon
- Amazon Advantage
- Amazon Webstore
- Checkout by Amazon

As you check out each one, use the Your Notes section below to write down the main points of each one, or, if you join, write down your username and password. Follow what the program suggests and begin making money.

13.2. Your Notes

Another option for using this section is to write down a list of products you have on hand that you could sell on Amazon so you can research if those items are available.

14.0. Start Your Own Social Media Site

What better way to make money online than to create your own social media site. Why do Facebook and Twitter have all the traffic? If you should start a social media site, and promote it properly, you can make money off it like those big guys do. Mark Zuckerberg first created Facebook with two other friends while in college.

If you know nothing about setting up such a site, hire someone to do it for you. That person can create the site the way you want it. Then offer a free trial for a week or two weeks, so people can get a feel for what it looks like and how it works. Then, bill their credit card after the trial period is over. If you don't charge a membership fee, you can always seek advertisers. This is how

Facebook makes so much money. They charge people a certain amount to place ads on their network. Facebook makes millions from those ads, and you can do it, too.

Here is a list of places where you can use to create your own social media site:

1. http://www.mixxt.net/
2. http://www.spruz.com/
3. http://www.ning.com/
4. http://wall.fm/
5. http://www.socialgo.com/

Each site has step-by-step directions for how to get your social media site up and operational in seconds.

Social media is here to stay. Every time you turn around someone has created another social site. Why not capitalize on it and make money yourself? Get on the bandwagon and create one of your own.

14.1. Action Plan

For this activity, go to each website as listed
below and check to see what they can offer
you. If it appeals to you, take the next step.
If you don't like the setup or terms, move
on to the next one.

1. http://www.mixxt.net/
2. http://www.spruz.com/
3. http://www.ning.com/
4. http://wall.fm/
5. http://www.socialgo.com/

14.2. Your Notes

Write down a list of the websites you visited
and the ones you decided to work with. This
will help you keep track. If you chose to
ignore a site, note the reason why so you
won't go back to it again.

By keeping yourself organized, it will help you in the end as you work the programs and make money.

15.0. Write Articles for Profit

Can you write? If you have a knack for using words in the right way and order, you may find a niche as an article writer. There is a constant need for web content. Many website and blog owners are always on the lookout for content. If you write well and fast enough, you will find many that pay well for content.

Unfortunately, there are some people who think writing is nothing. They are only willing to pay $1 to $5 for 300 to 400 words. As someone said on LinkedIn recently, there are those who respect writers enough to pay them well for article writing, and you only have to work for the ones you choose.

One way to make money with your writing is by writing for companies that sell your writing over and over again.

Here is a list of companies that will pay writers to create articles for them:

1. Helium.com
2. eHow.com
3. Triond.com
4. Hubpages.com
5. Suite101.com
6. Constant-Content.com
7. Textbroker.com
8. Xomba.com
9. Examiner.com
10. AssociatedContent.com
11. Ezinearticles.com
12. Bukisa.com
13. Squidoo.com
14. Gather.com
15. InternationalLiving.com

16. English.OhmyNews.com

17. SoftwareJudge.com

18. LovetoKnow.com

19. MethodShop.com

20. Howtodothings.com

21. TheDabblingMum.com

22. GroundReport.com

23. WireTapMag.org

24. AuctionBytes.com

25. About.com

26. DayTipper.com

27. DigitalJournal.com

28. LifeTips.com

29. ReviewStream.com

30. Shvoong.com

31. Epinions.com

32. LetterRep.com

33. Articlebase.com

Even if you aren't an exceptional writer, as long as you can write in a way that makes sense, you can create articles and make money off them. There are countless people doing this, even in foreign countries. Why should they get all the work? Go to the sites listed in this chapter and apply for an account. Once you have done so, find out what content they need and proceed to write it. You'll benefit in many ways. You will create content you like, you'll learn something new, and you'll teach others as well, not to mention being paid for it.

15.1. Action Plan

For this activity, go to each website I listed in this chapter:

Sign up for an account. Once your account is active, begin writing and submitting to them.

15.2. Your Notes

As you go through the list of sites above, if you come across any that are no longer active or have stopped publishing articles, make a note of them, and send an email to me on my website. When I update the book, I'll remove those sites that no longer work.

16.0. Make Money with Photography

If you are a photographer or have photos on your hard drive, you can make money from them. If you are a professional photographer, you can really make a ton of money online. However, if you are an amateur, have no fear, because you can also make good money online with your photos.

The key to selling photos online is to have photos that capture the interest of people. For instance, if you have a photo of a celebrity or the President, that picture will be worth many thousands of dollars.

You can get started selling online by going out and finding interesting or unique things or people and begin shooting images. Maybe you can capture someone doing

153

something that is unusual or not ordinary. Alternatively, maybe you can capture an event like Occupy Wall Street.

If you go to BigStockPhoto.com, they will allow you to upload your photo. When someone sees your photo and downloads it, you will earn $3 for that download. It may not be much, but think if a thousand people were to download that photo within a short time. You could earn over three thousand dollars before you know it.

This is not the only website that pays you for your photos. Here is a list of websites that also allows you to make money from your photos:

- ShutterPoint.com
- PhotoStockPlus.com
- FreelancePhotoJobs.com
- BigStockphoto.com
- 123RF.com

- ShutterShock.com
- StockPhotos.com
- CameraDollars.com
- Fotolia.com
- ShareAPic.net
- Break.com
- IstockPhoto.com

It really isn't hard to make money with your photos. You just need interesting looking photos and a place for them.

16.1. Action Plan

In this chapter, if you wish to call it that, there are a number of websites listed to help you sell your photography. In your action plan, go to each site, find one or more that you feel comfortable with, and upload any photos you have any available. Each website listed above has their rules regarding your photos. They also have their own payment system. That's why you have to take time, visit each one, and see what they offer and what their terms are.

As you learn of the hottest photos on the above sites, make note of them as well. By doing so, when you find yourself in such a situation, take a photo of it yourself, so you can improve your chances of making money from your photos. When you provide something that is interesting, informative, rouses curiosity, or simply grabs attention, you have created a situation where a sale will be forthcoming.

16.2. Your Notes

List the sites you joined, and the type of photos you have.

17.0. Real Estate Referrals

Do you know you can make money referring people to properties, without even seeing them? If you are a good researcher, and have connections with real estate brokers and agents, you can make money as a real estate referral agent.

The set up for this is simple. Put up a website that lets people know you are a real estate referral agent. On the website, mention that if people are looking for a certain property or piece of real estate, they can fill out a form or send an email with details about the property they are looking for. Charge the visitor a certain fee to find property certain number of properties matching their descriptions.

Once you get that information, along with your payment, you can send the information to your local real estate broker or agent, and let that person find the property for you. That person can then either send you the details or contact the visitor personally with the information.

Normally, you would contact a few agents and brokers in your area and ask if they will charge you a fee for providing information about a property to them. In a way, you can ask if they offer a finder's fee. If they do, you can make money for every person that you refer to them.

This is how the entire plan works. When you get a listing from someone on your website, you can charge that person for the request. Maybe you can charge the visitor anywhere from $25 to $150 as a processing fee, to find the property. Then you connect with the broker or agent. If he/she also provides you a finder's fee, you just collected perhaps $25 to $200, depending on the finder's fee. By the time you end the transaction, you made anywhere from $50 to $350. Not bad for a few hours of work.

Before you get into this, check with your state to see if you need a license. Some states require it, while other states don't.

In order to get people to come to your website, you just have to market it in the right places, Go online and find For-Sale-By-Owner (FSBO) postings. You can also go to auction sites, as well as HUD homes online.

Here are some sites that will get you going. These sites offer payment for leads, and also provide potential partners you can contact for referrals:

- ActiveRain.com
- Point2agent.com
- BiggerPockets.com

- RealTown.com
- InvestorsLoungeOnline.com
- Weichert.com/referralassociates
- ReferralNetworkInc.com
- ExitRealty.com

All you have to do is find the right partner to send referral leads to and create a good website to attract leads, and you can make good money.

17.1. Action Plan

To get started, contact your state and ask if you need a license to provide referrals for real estate transactions. Let them know you are acting as the middleman and connecting potential homeowners to agents or brokers for a finder's fee, and that you are collecting money from potential homebuyers as a professing fee. If there is no license involved, get busy building your website.

Once you have completed your website, the next step is to go to the websites listed in this chapter and connect with a partner or partners. Then go online and find For-Sale-By-Owner (FSBO) postings. You can also go to auction sites, as well as HUD homes online.

17.2. Your Notes

In this section, record the list of names you collect from your website. Also, write down your agent or broker's name so you can keep track of them. You may also want to keep track of how many homes you referred on a daily basis.

18.0. Build Websites

There are many people who see the Internet as a goldmine of opportunity. If you have any skill in website creation, or have some web design software, you could help these companies and individuals get online by creating a website for them. Nowadays, with the popularity of WordPress, getting online is much easier. It is just a matter of installing WordPress and setting it up, then creating the content that needs to be put in place.

All you have to do is tell people that you are an expert (you don't have to be) in using WordPress, and you would like to help them get their site set up. You can charge them an hourly fee or a flat rate fee. That choice is yours.

Once you have done the work, you can charge them a monthly fee to keep their site updated and maintained. You would be surprised how many people would jump to such an opportunity. Even if you don't install WordPress, as long as you have some kind of web design software, you can still create the web pages. The main thing you need is their graphics and content.

Some people charge per page. They find this is more lucrative for them. What you can also do is find a template that will fit the theme they want for their site and work with that.

If you have to pay for the theme, you can be reimbursed when you charge them your web design fee.

If you'd rather find templates to download for use as you create web pages, here are a few sites that provide templates:

- WebsiteSource.com
- TemplateMonster.com
- FreeWebsiteTemplates.com
- Steves-Templates.com
- BuyTemplates.net
- TemplatesBox.com
- BoxedArt.com
- FreeLayouts.com
- eCrater.com
- Homestead.com

Although there are many people doing this work, if you offer people something unique to go along with your web design service, you'll be able to gather more business and beat your competition.

18.1. Action Plan

To get started, look and see if you have any web design software. Some designers use Coffee Cup. Some use Dreamweaver. It depends on how much you know about

HTML and web design. If you don't know much about HTML, it may be a good idea to invest in an HTML editor that provides you with a WYSIWYG system.

Go to the sites provided in this chapter and find templates you can use for various types of web designs. If you have to sign up to use the site, do it.

Decide in advance whether to offer website by using WordPress or by using an HTML editor and downloading readymade templates. Each template is structured for that particular theme or industry.

Once you have decided on the design software, platform, and gathered templates, the next step is to create your own website where you let people know about your services. Make sure to really beef it up, as it will be the showcase for your work.

After you have completed your website, the next step is to advertise for clients. You can do this by way of social media sites for the time being.

18.2. Your Notes

In this section, why not write the pros and cons of using WordPress or your own HTML editor. You may have to wait until you get some jobs before you actually decide. This way you'll know which method you need to focus on.

Use the space below for your thoughts.

19.0. Online Game Developer

Are you presently a programmer? If you are, do you see yourself an online game developer? If you don't have it now, you may have to invest in some special software that allows you to create video games.

The people who are already creating online games not only have fun creating them, but are raking in the money as well. Online games can range from simple to complex. All it takes is an idea and the software.

You can gather ideas by visiting online forums and certain organizations. The average online game developer can make about $68,000 a year or more. In fact, some game developers have been known to make up to $150,000. You don't even need a lot of experience. Just have patience, determination, and time to learn how to use the software, along with some creativity, of course.

If you are truly a video game enthusiast, or like playing games online, why not put your interests to good use.

Here are some sites you can look at that can get you started as an online game developer:

- GameRecruiter.com: This is a professional recruiting organization with a staff possessing many years of experience in the interactive game industry. They can help you get work as an online game developer.
- GameJobs.com: This is the leading employment site serving the game industry. You will find work and resources to help get you started as a game developer.

- GameDaily.com: This is the game industries number one source for daily news.
- TigSource.com: This is an independent gaming news blog. You can learn of the latest developments in gaming, where to find the right software, and where to find work.
- MadMonkey.net: This site lists newly developed games. They also provide resources you can use as well as a way for you to promote any game you create.
- IndieGamer.com: This is an online forum for independent game developers.
- IndieGames.com: This is a news blog for independent game developers to keep you updated on what is happening in the world of online games.

- IndieGameJobs.com: This website posts jobs for online game developers.
- MakingIndieGames.com: This site provides resources and instructions on how to develop games online and how to use various game creation software.
- IndieGameTools.com: This website provides information and reviews on the tools needed to develop games.
- GameDev.net: This website provides information on jobs, tools, news, and help for beginners.
- Direct2Drive.com: This website promotes new online games.
- GameDeveloperCareers.com: This is an online job board for the game industry.

- AnimationArena.com: This website provides job links and schools that teach game design.
- Gamasutra.com: On this site, you will learn the art and business side of creating online games.

It doesn't take much to enter this field. If you are a programmer, you'll be able to get in much faster. However, if you are not, you can still work the field. You may have to get a reference guide or programming guide to use as you create your programs. If you have a logical mind and understand how computers work, you'll have no problem going into the online game developer field.

If you have no clue about programming, or how online video games work, you will have either to skip this, or take a course in video game programming first. You can't develop programs if you don't know how they work and what makes them successful. You must understand the language and understand coding. Much of game development requires understanding how to program in high-level languages like C, C++, Java, and many others plus natural creativity and a sense of fun.

19.1. Action Plan

If you are presently a game developer or programmer, you are one step ahead of the game. If not, you will need to take steps to bring yourself up to speed. Visit the sites listed in this chapter and learn the requirements to be an online game developer. Once you understand what is involved, take the steps to secure the software and a manual, so you can learn about the online game world. This way you'll know what steps you need to take to succeed.

If you already know how to create games, begin to do the work and find companies to buy your games, using the website list I gave you in this chapter. If you don't know how to create games, research online and find out how to go about doing it. You can only succeed at online game development if you know the language used and what is required to create them.

19.2. Your Notes

Note below the steps that you need to take to learn what you need to do and how to do it. Your next step is to take action to accomplish those requirements. Following a step-by-step plan will help get you there.

20.0. Online Tutor

Do you have a special skill or talent? If you do, why not share it with others. The need for teachers and tutors is greater now than it ever has been. Despite the recession, people still need schooling and are willing to pay for it, as some people are being laid off their jobs and need to go into a new field or industry or learn new skills.

If you were to take time out and do a survey, you might discover something interesting. Business owners, housewives, and college students are discovering how great the Internet is for learning. Most universities and colleges are now providing online courses for both people who want to take special classes, and for those wanting to go for a degree.

It is for this reason that working as an online tutor can be a big opportunity for you. The number of people going online to study has increased dramatically over the years. What does this mean for you? If you are qualified to teach on a certain subject or two, you can make money by offering tutoring services.

Many people taking courses online are struggling to get through them the best way they can. Some of these courses are mandatory for the student to get his/her degree. If you know this particular subject, you can avail yourself of the knowledge you have and use it to help these students.

If you are looking to work as a tutor, you can create a website and advertise as a tutor. You can list the subjects you can tutor. The next thing is to promote your site. You can do this on Facebook, Twitter, and LinkedIn, to name a few places.

Besides your website, there are lists of sites you can join and work as a tutor for them. These sites are listed below:

- BrainyYack.com
- MyTutor24.com
- ETS.org
- Ed2Go.com
- WritingClasses.com
- UniversalClass.com
- Ether.com
- StudentofFortune.com
- Kasamba.com
- Ehow.com
- JustAnswer.com

Are you ready to tutor people? If you are, you can make good money online. Book the student and collect the money. How much easier can it be?

As long as you have something that no other person knows, or you have a new way of thinking about something that is old, you can tutor people and clean up. All it takes is building a website, advertising and promoting it, and then watching as people start contacting you on a regular basis for help.

In addition to being a tutor, you can also score test results at home. ETS is one big supplier of testing. They employ people scoring tests for them at your home.

20.1. Action Plan

If you know a subject that is in demand right now, you can tutor those that are trying to learn it. Why not help those that are stepping up to the plate to learn new skills. Take the plunge and go to the above websites. Register for each one, or take your pick. Then create a nice profile. Once you have completed that, wait for the students to start contacting you.

In the meantime, you can also set up a website where you offer tutoring services. By offering your services through your website, you can reach many people. You won't have to depend on local clients to teach. You can stretch your client base across a global arena. Just make sure that the students you teach understand English if this is your primary language.

20.2. Your Notes

Write down the subjects you know a lot about and then research online to find out if there is a demand for teachers or tutors for those subjects. Check the sites I listed in this chapter. If here is a demand, you have struck gold.

21.0. Create Membership Sites

Do you know the number one sites that make continuous money are membership sites? That's right. Many marketers and business people, who run membership sites, claim they make good money each month or every six months.

If you are good or at least decent at creating websites, you can make a great deal of money creating a membership site. Membership sites are built so that when people come to look at content, they have to log in first. Before they can log in, they have to register and pay a fee to do so. This fee will be monthly, three months, six months, or a year.

The one downside to a membership site is that the owner has to keep adding content to the site. If the owner doesn't add new content every day or every week, people that have signed up for membership, will cancel and not come back.

If you believe you have an idea that people will be glad to pay for on a regular basis, perhaps it would be a great idea to have a membership site.

To learn more about how to create a membership site and what it involves, here are some sites to help you:

- http://membershipsiteadvisor.com/
- http://www.squidoo.com/membership-website
- http://www.johnchow.com/how-to-start-a-money-making-membership-site-part-1/
- http://www.johnchow.com/how-to-start-a-money-making-membership-site-part-2/

- http://www.membershipacademy.com/member/login.php
- http://www.slideshare.net/JeremyGislason/how-to-start-a-membership-site-that-makes-you-money

You can also create a membership site with WordPress. WordPress has a plug-in that allows for many levels of security and memberships.

To learn more about this go to this website: http://www.webbriefcase.net/2009-04/building-a-membership-site-with-wordpress/

If you follow the advice as found in this chapter, you will be able to adapt a membership site that you can run for a long time. Just keep in mind that when you start such a site, you had better have really good content available or people will lose interest, and you don't want that to happen.

186

21.1. Action Plan

If you know a subject that is in demand right now, create a membership site based on that subject. If you are unsure how to go about creating the site, go to each site listed in this chapter for advice on what you need to do, then take action.

Get your membership site started. If you use WordPress, get the plugin. Once everything is in place, begin promoting the site. Within a short time, you will begin making money.

21.2. Your Notes

In this section, write down the subjects you know well and check to see if there is a demand for them. Go to Google and type in a keyword that represents your subject. If there are a few sites available, you have found a good subject or niche.

22.0. Sell Tools to Social Media Users

If you keep up with the latest trends, you know that social media is the hottest trend online. Millions of users flock to such sites as Facebook, Twitter, LinkedIn, Digg, and many others. The one aspect to Facebook you may find interesting is that they use tools. People can sign up and use add-on tools to improve their online experience. When you go to a social media site, they try to get you to use tools to make your use of the social site easier, more productive, and more entertaining.

Why not take advantage of the popularity of social media by creating tools. You can charge per tool or have it set up as a shopping cart system. Whichever way you arrange it, you can make money by offering

189

tools to those that want to use social media and get the best use of the sites.

Here are some tools that you may want to offer people:

1. Cinches: Go to CinchCast.com. This tool can record audio for you. You can record via the Internet or by phone. Many people like this tool and use it regularly when they want to record and share such recordings.

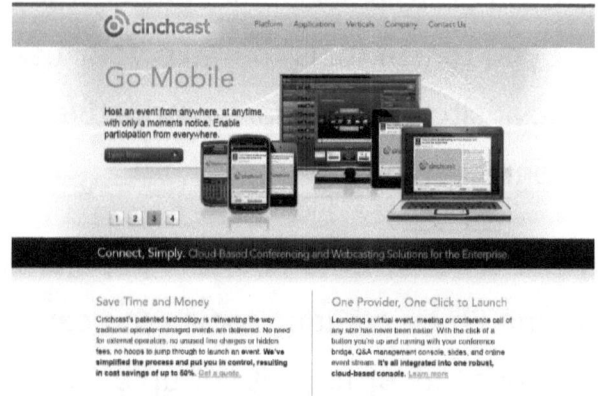

2. Screenr: This tool allows you to create screen-captured video that includes audio. The software is easy to use. You can record and pause the video at any time. When you are ready, just click "Done."

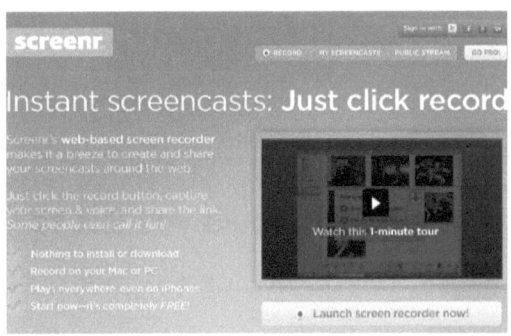

3. Postling: This tool brings all the social media sites together into one interface. When someone leaves a comment on a social site, you automatically get an email notification of that comment.

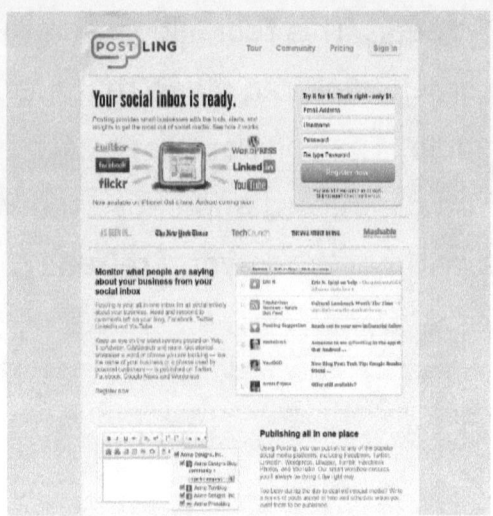

4. Inside View: Would you like to know who it is you are dealing with on a professional level? With Inside View, you can. Simply type in the name of the person you are looking at and you can extract valuable information about the person, including personal and business information.

5. OnlyWire: With OnlyWire, you can have your blog post auto-submitted to up to 42 top social network sites. Such sites can include Digg, Reddit, and StumbleUpon to name a few.

6. TweetDeck: TweetDeck is one of the most famous and often used social media tools. You can combine Twitter, Facebook, and other social sites into one tool. This way you don't have to monitor those sites. Just run TweetDeck and get your posts and comments into one place. TweetDeck became so popular that Twitter itself bought it.

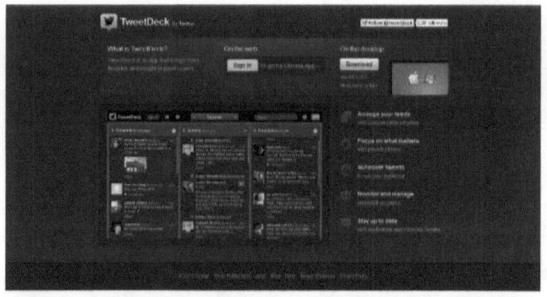

Most of the tools listed on this page are free, but there are some that you have to pay to use. What better way to make money online than by offering something that people can take advantage of and use? People will be more than willing to pay to use such tools, if they help make their lives better.

22.1. Action Plan

Do you have access to tools and apps that will help other people enjoy more fully their social media experience? If so, offer the apps for sale. If you don't, why not go to the sites I listed in this chapter and sign up to sell one of the tools listed. At least this way you can get your hands into it and start making money.

22.2. Your Notes

Write down all the apps or tools you have. If you currently don't have any, go to the sites in this chapter and evaluate what each one has. Then write down the tools and apps you may be interested in selling or promoting.

You can use as many as you want, as long as you are able to keep track of them. It is when you get too many that you could lose track of what you have and what you are selling.

23.0. Write a Newsletter

Do you subscribe to a newsletter? There are two different types – One that you get in the mail and one you get in your inbox. The former is simply a newsletter, but the latter is referred to as an e-zine. There are tons of e-zines online. There are more e-zines than there are print versions of newsletters.

If you have something important to say and you know there's a market for it, you can create a newsletter that people will be willing to pay to get. The newsletters that come to your mailbox are examples of paid newsletters. They are probably about 10 – 20 pages long. They are often delivered once or twice a month.

If you are interested in providing a newsletter to people, and want it to be a paid subscription, you better make sure your information is top-notch and something people haven't heard or read before. It can be a new twist on something done before, or it could be a completely new discovery. Whatever it is, as long as it is new and has a lot of value to it, people will be willing to pay for it.

If you go to websites that provide newsletters you can be sent to your home, you may find that they may offer monthly or yearly subscriptions that are paid in advance. These are the most popular types.

There are also newsletters that are given out to those that subscribe. These are e-zines and are usually free; however, there are select ones you have to pay for.

To start a newsletter is rather easy. All you have to do is simply create a website where you advertise the newsletter, and when people visit the site, allow them to purchase their subscription online. You can also send a flyer in the Sunday edition of your local newspaper, letting people know about your newsletter.

You can buy a list, and send them a postcard with your website address on it, or provide them with a return postcard with credit card info on it. This way you can run the credit card through and send them the newsletter by mail. Setting up this kind of newsletter can be costly, as you have to pay for printing and mailing costs. What would be cheaper is to offer your subscribers the option to get the newsletter by email instead. No cost will be associated with the e-e-newsletter except for the subscription fee.

No matter how you work it, this is no doubt one of the best methods of making money there is. Just make sure you have something good that people want to read about. Make sure to keep the price for the newsletter down low so people can afford it.

23.1. Action Plan

Come up with some ideas for a newsletter. Search the Internet to see if there is a demand for such an idea. If you do find a demand, create a five or ten page newsletter. Put up a website advertising this newsletter. Keep the cost of the newsletter down for now to see how many subscriptions you can get.

After a while, you may want to streamline that newsletter into an e-zone format, and offer that for free or a small fee. Then you can give your subscribers a choice of the printed newsletter or the e-zine. Before long, you will begin making a lot of money.

23.2. Your Notes

Use this space to record the ideas you come up with for your newsletter. When you write down your ideas, think of different ways to express your idea and write them down as well.

24.0. Make Money Doing Research

Are you good at research? Can you find something quickly? Do you have the inside track, as it were, to find things that people can't normally find with ease. If you are really a great researcher, you can make a ton of money.

Business people are constantly looking for information about competitors or the newest trends in Internet marketing. If you can find the information these business people need, they will be more than willing to pay you handsomely for it. I get emails very often for companies looking for a researcher for various reasons.

You can make a ton of money online by researching and finding statistics, facts, or quotes for individuals that need them. It really isn't that hard to make money online as a researcher. You just need to let people know you are skilled and available.

Perhaps you can put up a website that announces your research services. Request that people fill out a form, stating what they need, then click a payment button and pay for the research, or send you the form by email. Once you get the form, you can contact them and let them know the cost involved. After they've paid for your services, you can proceed onward with doing their research.

If you promote yourself properly, before you know it, you'll have so much business you won't know what to do with it. You may have to find someone to help you. You can learn new things and find things that you didn't think existed and be paid for doing it.

If you want to get started fast, why not go to websites like Elance.com or GetAFreelancer.com and post that you are a researcher. This way you can build up a client base pretty quickly. You don't have to settle for those sites. You can also go on LinkedIn and let people know, by way of your profile, that you are a researcher. You may be surprised just how many clients you can get this way.

24.1. Action Plan

For this exercise, go online to Indeed.com (http://www.indeed.com), Google Alerts (http://www.google.com/alerts), and SimplyHired.com (http://www.simplyhired.com). Select Researcher jobs or research jobs as the keywords. You'll come up with a list almost immediately on Indeed.com and SimplyHired.com.

24.2. Your Notes

Write down the exact keywords you use and monitor how many ads you receive from Indeed.com, Google Alert, and SimplyHired that feature researcher jobs and/or research jobs for those keywords. If you find you get more leads by using one keyword combination or by itself, focus on those keywords. You don't want to get repeated job leads. This is why you have to monitor them both to see which type of job is more in common.

In some cases, the researcher jobs may focus on the need for a researcher to do some kind of project. In others, you may discover that an ad with research jobs may only require a person to come in and help with many duties including research. Read the ads carefully.

25.0. Language Translation Service

Do you know many different languages? Are you fluent in Spanish, French, Italian, or German? If you know more than one language, why not offer your services as a language translator.

Language translators are used very often to decipher documents and translate them from one language to another. You don't even need to know those languages. There is software you can purchase that will take one language and translate it into another.

If you really would like to take advantage of this market, it would be beneficial to investigate it more fully. Find out what software is available to use for translation. You may be able to get the software cheap, if you look hard enough and do research.

There are also websites that offer translations for free (just don't tell your client that). Google has such a translation service, but not many people know about it.

Why miss an opportunity to help people take documents and translate them from one language to another, when you can make a lot of money doing it? It just takes letting people know which languages you can translate and the amount you charge. Before long, you'll be very busy.

Just create a website where you list the languages you can translate from and to. That is really all that matters. You can accept payment ahead of time, or accept payment when the work has been completed.

If you are really good with different languages, you may not even need language translation software, as you can do the translation yourself.

Here is a link to a site that provides reviews of translation software, so you can choose the one that may be right for you:

http://translation-software-review.toptenreviews.com/

25.1. Action Plan

For this exercise, write down a list of the languages you know, and go online to find out if there is language translation software that can translate that language into another one. If you do find it, investigate to see if it is worth a purchase, unless you can get it as a free trial.

On the other hand, if you really do know other languages well, just take what documents you have and translate them based on what you know. It may be advisable to have a dictionary available in case you aren't sure about the proper spelling of a word.

25.2. Your Notes

Take the list of languages and find a document on your hard drive. Use the space below to translate one sentence or paragraph from one language to another. This will give you some practice. Make sure that when you translate, you do so in various languages, not just one.

Once you have completed this section, you should have created a few sentences or short paragraphs in different languages.

26.0. Make Money with Online Dating

Did you know that dating sites are one of the biggest attractors for people today? Men and women go online to find a date or to establish a relationship with someone. No one really wants to be lonely, unless that person is a hermit.

If you have been to dating sites like Match.com, Speeddating.com, OKCupid.com, and many other sites, take a look at the way they are set up. They may offer certain services for free, but if you want to contact the person, you would have to pay a premium.

Owners of dating sites can make up to $1000 and more a day. This depends on how the site is promoted, and the amount paid for the memberships.

For example, Speeddating.com offers you a chance to browse and have a chat with a woman for only two minutes. After that, if you wish to continue, you will have to upgrade to the monthly fee, which is about $24.95, or somewhere in that range.

Imagine if 100 people were to land on the site and register. The owner just got paid $2495.00 for one day. Do you see the potential? If you have the right system in place, and work it correctly, you can make a lot of money, and have few maintenance costs.

If you want to learn more about how to set up a dating website, click here: http://www.diy-dating.com/.

Why not dig deep into this area and find out what is required to start a dating site? Every day an entrepreneur gets hold of

213

venture capital and starts a dating site. Why not do the same yourself?

It is important to do research online regarding creating a dating website. There are many online now. If you want to have a piece of the pie, you need to find out what they don't offer that you can.

Once your website has been completed, you can take steps to promote it. By doing this, people will begin flocking to your site. If they like what they see, they will sign up and begin using it. When you have a huge following, venture capitalists will be more than willing to give you the money you need.

26.1. Action Plan

To get started, go to the website shown above and learn what is required to start a dating site. Once you know the details, follow each step one-by-one. Once you have followed through and know exactly what steps you have to take to start a dating website, take the next step by going online and finding a venture capital firm that is willing to back you up.

26.2. Your Notes

In this section, write down the steps you need in order to build a dating website. After you write them down, follow through. Also, write down a list of venture capital people in your area. Take out a big piece of paper, or use Word, and create a business plan for a website startup. Here is a document to help get you started: http://www.connect.org/resources/docs/Springboard_Business_Plan_Guide.pdf.

Extra Tidbits

Here are some extra tidbits I would like to throw at you. These extra facts will help you as you seek to achieve greatness with each niche you work.

Effective Website

The first step is to create a simple but effective website. Don't make it extravagant, just a simple site that describes your product or service clearly. Emphasize the benefits of your product or service. Look at your copy and answer this question: Does it answer your customer's pressing problems in ten seconds or less? If not, you need to revise it accordingly.

Basically, when people arrive at your site, they are looking to do something. If they don't see any action to take, they will leave.

It only takes five to six seconds for them to make up their mind.

Make sure the navigation is easy and you have a contact page listed. Also, check the keywords you use for your site or page. If you don't have the keyword listed in the right place, nothing will happen. You won't be indexed.

Blogging

I spoke about this earlier in this book, but I wanted to mention blogging here, from a different point of view. Previously, you were told you could make good money from your blog. What I want to state here is that you can get good ranking from your blog based on the comments you post. All you have to do is put certain keywords in your post and when Google indexes your blog, they will categorize it based on those keywords.

Also, when you post comments, be conversational in tone. This lets people know you are human. What better way to draw a lot of visitors and readers than by showing your personal side instead of just your business side?

Podcasting

Podcasting was not mentioned in this book, but you can make money with it. You can create a podcast of an event or show, place it on your website, and sell it to subscribers for a certain low fee. Many people do this and have done quite well.

If you have recording and editing equipment, use a microphone and record whatever you want. Make sure to speak clearly in the microphone so people can hear you. Speak slowly so your words are easy to understand.

218

Edit your recording to take out any outside or distracting noise. You only want your voice to be heard in the recording, nothing else. Once you have taken that step, you are done. Just upload it and before long, you will begin getting subscribers.

YouTube

Did you know you can make money if your video is on YouTube? I mentioned in this book that one niche is on video recording. If you take your recording, place it on YouTube.com, and promote it, before long, people will come to the page on YouTube.com to view your recording. They can even give your video feedback. If they like what they see, they can send the link to your video to their friends. Their friends can do likewise.

If you really want your videos to go viral quickly, the best way to do this is by using

219

YouTube.com. Many entrepreneurs and marketers have used YouTube.com in the past to make money and have done very well at it. Why not do the same yourself?

Just follow the rules YouTube.com established for making videos and you will soon create a following.

I hope you get as much joy out of this book as I had in writing it. Use what you read in this book and make money. You deserve to.

Summary

As you read the many pages of this document, you learned many ways to make money online. These are niches that have proven to make a ton of money for those who have worked them. Some niches are easy while others are not; some are very lucrative, some are not.

The best advice I can give you is to work each niche and see how it goes. If you do well, continue with it. Why not work with several niches. If you create and work with more than one niche, you can have multiple streams of income.

The best way to begin is to start with the first one and get that working. Once you have it down and are making money with it, go on to the next one and repeat the procedure. Before you know it, you'll have many streams of income.

Above all else, the method you try should not be a bore to you. It should be fun to engage in. If you don't enjoy what you are trying to do, you won't make it work. You have to work at it, but you should also have fun with the process. I was told that when you are having fun doing something, you succeed better at it. I believe this goes for work to.

Don't let what you do become a source of frustration or pain. Instead, take pleasure in what you do and take pride in your ability to accomplish your goal.

Once you choose your method, set it up, and promote it heavily. You will benefit and end up making good money online. Remember: as you work the niches, be patient. You may not make a lot of money right away, but you will in time. Just show up and work the system. The money will follow.